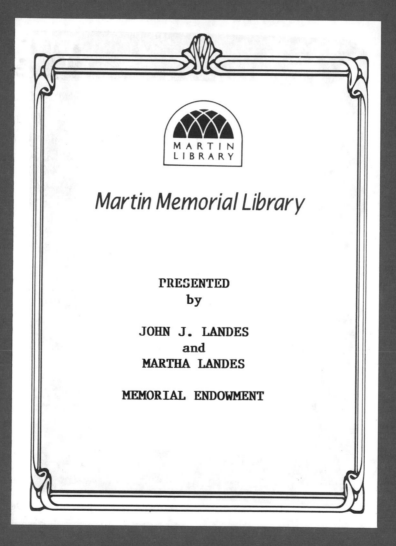

This early valentine states, "Upon this little Valentine, Your name I have inscribed with care; If you could look within my heart, You'd find the same name written there." Marked, "Whitney Made Worcester Mass."

GREETINGS
with LOVE

GREETINGS
with LOVE
The Book of
Valentines

Michele Karl

PELICAN PUBLISHING COMPANY
Gretna 2003

The word "Pelican" and the depiction of a pelican are trademarks
of Pelican Publishing Company, Inc., and are registered
in the U.S. Patent and Trademark Office.

Library of Congress Cataloging-in-Publication Data

Karl, Michele.
  Greetings with love : the book of valentines / Michele Karl.
      p. cm.
Includes bibliographical references.
  ISBN 1-56554-993-7 (hardcover : alk. paper)
  1. Valentines—Collectors and collecting—Catalogs. 2. Valentine's
Day—History. I. Title.
  NC1866.V3 K37 2003
  394.2618'0973'075—dc21
                                                        2002007314

Printed in China
Published by Pelican Publishing Company, Inc.
1000 Burmaster Street, Gretna, Louisiana 70053

CONTENTS

The poem reads, "Well I know your friends are many For the world's in love with you. But I'd give a bright new penny Just to know you like me, too." Inscribed, "To Gena Mae Elliott from Pauline Elliott." Maker unknown, 1936.

PROLOGUE

I have always been a collector of one thing or another. I started my collection with dolls, then added children's books, costume jewelry, and Marilyn Monroe items. Somewhere along the way I began collecting old paper items, mainly postcards and photographs. I tended toward cupids and love themes with children shown in the image. Before I knew it, I was collecting valentines. I began to accumulate vintage valentine postcards and other ephemera. Throughout these pages you will have the opportunity to see the wonderful images of children at play, lovers embracing, and love that have brought me much joy.

Valentine's Day. These words alone conjure up thoughts of young love, chocolates, and red roses. This holiday for lovers has been embraced by today's civilization as the one day of the year reserved for that special someone. However, Valentine's Day is more than just a day for lovers. It is a day to show *anyone* you care about that they are special by giving tokens such as cards, flowers, candy, and gifts.

I will share folklore and rituals in these pages. I will present old-fashioned as well as modern-day Valentine's Day traditions in a beautiful array of poems, recipes, crafts, and other expressions of love.

Greetings with Love: The Book of Valentines is a collection of love messages expressed through postcards, valentine cards, and other printed matter. My hope is that, as you read this book, it will bring you the same pleasure that I experienced in writing it.

Enjoy!

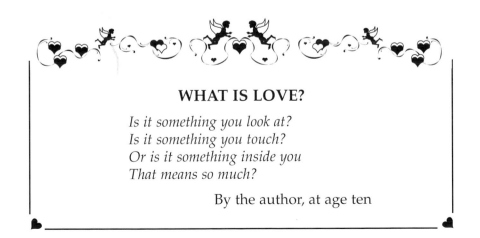

WHAT IS LOVE?

Is it something you look at?
Is it something you touch?
Or is it something inside you
That means so much?

By the author, at age ten

This valentine from the 1950s states, "Valentine Thoughts of You" on the cover. The inside reads, "It makes no difference where I go, No matter what I do, Through the flying daylight hours My thoughts are all of you; And when the little stars appear And silv'ry moonlight gleams, I close my eyes in sleep, and then—I see you in my dreams!" Marked, "Rust Craft Boston U.S.A."

INTRODUCTION

How do I love thee? Across the world, February 14 is marked as the one day to show the one you love how much you care. There are so many ways to demonstrate love. Some show it by giving candy, flowers, and gifts to loved ones, friends, and family. This is all done, of course, in the name of St. Valentine. Who is this saint? And why do we celebrate this day? As you read on, you will learn the customs and legends of this special day, from its earliest beginnings to the Valentine's Day traditions of today.

Here are some fun valentine facts. Did you know the number of United States places with "heart" in their names is four? Yet there were not many hearts in these towns! The census for 2000 showed fewer than 1,000 people in each of these locales: Heart Butte, Montana; Sacred Heart, Minnesota; South Heart, North Dakota; and Heartwell, Nebraska. The number of places in the United States named Valentine is only two. Valentine, Nebraska, is the more populous of the two, with 2,820 residents; Valentine, Texas, has just 187. The number of places nationwide with "love" in their name is nine. Loveland, Colorado, is the most populous, according to the 2000 census, with 50,608 residents. The others are Lovejoy, Georgia; Lovelady, Texas; Loveland, Oklahoma; Loveland, Ohio; Loveland Park, Ohio; Lovelock, Nevada; Loves Park, Illinois; and Love Valley, North Carolina.

St. Valentine Greeting postcard. Unmarked and undated.

GREETINGS
with LOVE

"To Greet You My Valentine." This valentine is signed, *"Dear Mearl, Wishing you happiness and prosperity. Lovingly Miss Nelle."* Marked, *"Stecher Lith. Co. Roch. N.Y."*

HISTORY AND LEGENDS

Valentine's Day is not a legal holiday, which means that schools, post offices, and other offices are open. Still, it is a special day for people to celebrate, and celebrate they do! In countries near and far, an array of gifts is given on February 14, including flowers, candy, and, last but not least, Valentine's Day cards, better known simply as "valentines." Valentines are cards that can be purchased or made with loving hands. Most bear a message such as "To my loving husband" or "To a great friend." But before we go more in depth into what a valentine is, let us see where it all began.

The history and folklore of Valentine's Day, the day for lovers, is varied. How did it all begin? Who is this mysterious saint, and why do we celebrate this holiday? The answers to these questions can be found on the following pages.

February has been a month of romance for years. Valentine's Day is a mixture of both Christian and Roman traditions. The Catholic Church recognizes not one but at least three different saints named Valentine or Valentinus.

Some say that St. Valentine was a priest during the third century in Rome when Emperor Claudius II thought that single men made better fighters and soldiers than married men. So the emperor outlawed marriage for young men in order to increase his pick of soldiers. St. Valentine, refusing to obey the emperor, performed marriages anyway until Claudius finally put him to death.

St. Valentine as a priest and physician is one

"Sweetheart Be My Valentine." This embossed card is inscribed, "Happy Valentine From Grace Rohrer—Miss Zanerian Funk 102 Fairground Ave. City." It is postmarked Hagerstown, Maryland, February 13, 1912. Maker unknown.

"I send you this card and call you mine and love you always my valentine." Marked, "P.C. 245" and inscribed, "From Walter Harold Howley."

of the most popular legends. He was a kind-hearted doctor who practiced medicine in a small room in his home. St. or Dr. Valentine also loved to cook and would carefully prepare medicines that pleased his patients' taste buds. Many of his medicines contained honey, wines, or milk. He would lead followers in prayer. Many times he would pray for the good health of his patients. One day a jailer for the emperor of Rome knocked at Valentine's door holding his blind daughter in his arms. The tales of Valentine's medical and spiritual healing abilities had reached this man and he wanted desperately to find a cure for his daughter. After several visits and a number of weeks had passed, the girl's sight still had not been restored. Finally, soldiers arrived at the home of St. Valentine and arrested him. Before Valentine's execution date of February 14, he jotted his farewell message to the blind girl and signed it, "From your Valentine." When the blind girl opened the letter she was able to read St. Valentine's words—her eyesight was restored.

The legends continue. For instance, others believe that Emperor Claudius II arrested St. Valentine for helping Christian martyrs. After refusing to give up the Christian faith, he was beaten to death on February 14.

United States and British history differs from Roman and Catholic legends. It is said that while the Romans were conquering most of Europe, they brought valentines with them. They gave these messages of love to women they met.

Although the truth behind the Valentine legends is shadowy, many stories certainly emphasize Valentine's appeal as a sympathetic, heroic, and, most importantly, romantic figure. It is no surprise to many that by the Middle Ages, Valentine was one of the most popular saints in England and France.

It is really quite funny how many different legends there are about St. Valentine. Many are very similar yet have distinct features all their own. Any of the above explanations may be true. I think that Valentine's Day developed out of a combination of all or parts of the legends explained.

FEBRUARY 14

While some believe that Valentine's Day is celebrated in the middle of February to commemorate the anniversary of Valentine's death or burial—which probably occurred around A.D. 270—others believe that the Christian church may have decided to celebrate Valentine's feast day in the middle of February in an effort to "Christianize" celebrations of the pagan Lupercalia festival.

It is said that in A.D. 496, Pope Gelasius set aside February 14 as a day to honor St. Valentine. Valentine would become known as the patron saint of epilepsy, having suffered from it in life. He also became the patron saint of lovers when the church assimilated the fertility festival into its calendar.

In ancient Rome, February was the official beginning of spring and was considered a time for purification. Houses would be cleansed by sweeping them out and then sprinkling salt and a type of wheat called spelt throughout its interior. Lupercalia, which began February 15, was a fertility festival dedicated to Faunus, the Roman god of agriculture, as well as to the Roman founders Romulus and Remus. To begin the festival, members of the Luperci, an order of Roman priests, would gather at the sacred cave where the infants Romulus and

"Your Valentine sends her best wishes." Marked, "Series No. 9017. The Pink of Perfection Regd. The Fairman Co, Cin. & N.Y."

Remus were believed to have been taken care of by a she-wolf or *lupa*. The priests would then sacrifice a dog, for purification, and a goat, for fertility. The priests then sliced the goat's hide into strips, dipped them in the sacrificial blood, and took to the streets. They gave them to young men, who would gently slap both women and fields of crops with the goat-hide strips. You would think it would send terror through the women of the area. Instead, it was welcomed, since Roman women believed that being touched with the hides would make them more fertile in the year to come.

Later in the day, according to the legend, all the young women in the city would place their names in a big urn or bin. This ritual was known as "drawing lots." The city's bachelors would then each have a chance to choose a name out of the urn and become paired for the year with that chosen woman. These matches often ended in marriage. This custom was Christianized and spread throughout Europe and England. Later, the names drawn were of saints instead of girls, and the girls who drew the names were supposed to model those saints' behavior for the year, acting as well as

"Ye Valentine Wish. Apart, will we Surely be Lonely: Love me 'Cause I love thee Only." Marked, "S. Bergman N.Y. 1913."

they could. This change was not very popular, however.

In France the tradition differed. The first young man seen by a girl on Valentine's Day was to become her boyfriend, or valentine, for the year to come. It was expected for an engagement to follow at the end of the year, and in many cases, it did.

After Pope Gelasius declared February 14 St. Valentine's Day, the Roman "lottery" system for romantic pairing was found to be un-Christian and outlawed. Later, during the Middle Ages, it was believed in France and England that February 14 was the beginning of birds' mating season, which added to the idea that the middle of February—Valentine's Day—should be a time for love and romance (see "On the Wings of a Dove" chapter).

It is also thought that when Oliver Cromwell, Lord Protector of the Commonwealth, came to power he declared Valentine's Day immoral and had valentines banned. By 1660, Valentine's Day was restored. The 1969 book *The Valentine and Its Origins* states that the earliest valentine recorded in Britain contained verses of Chaucer. Chaucer served as an esquire in the royal court.

"To My Valentine:—Hands up! I'm playing robber, My weapon's cupid's dart, And I will keep you at its point Till you give me your heart." Maker unknown.

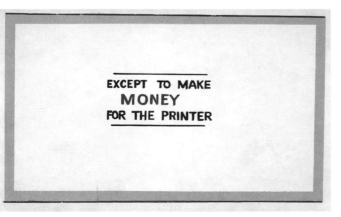

Some cards seem quite silly, such as this one, which states, "This valentine card has NO purpose . . . except to make money for the printer." Marked, "Valentine No. 15 Printed in U.S.A. © CVC."

"To My Valentine—I would be Friends with you and have your Love. Shakespear." Marked, "6718" and inscribed, "With love From Veora Patterson. Ruth Collins, City."

"To my Love." Inscribed, "Dear Aunt & Mama," with message, signed, "Your Little Niece Shirley." Dated 1949.

VALENTINE'S DAY CARD

The oldest known valentine still in existence was a poem written by a Frenchman, Charles, Duke of Orleans. It was sent to his wife while he was imprisoned in the Tower of London following his capture at the Battle of Agincourt. The greeting, which was written in 1415, is on view today at the British Museum in London, England. It is believed that several years later, King Henry V hired a writer named John Lydgate to compose a valentine note to Catherine of Valois.

Valentine's Day began to be widely celebrated there around the seventeenth century. Some say the Germans began the valentine tradition by sending *Freundschaftkarten* or "Friendship Cards" on the New Year, birthdays, and anniversaries. This custom was then imported to England and America in the 1700s, where such cards were given on Valentine's Day. Valentines were placed on friends' doorsteps and given to men and women in England while children sang valentine carols. By the middle of the eighteenth century, it was very common for friends and lovers from all social classes to exchange small gifts or handwritten notes.

This beautiful embossed valentine states, "To One I Fondly Love" and is signed, "To Mary from N. F."

"Roses are red, violets are blue, I'll always be warmhearted toward you." This card has a bow and heart in red raised fuzz.

"I have met many, Liked a few. Loved but one, Here's to you." Marked, "Authorized by act of Congress—May 19, 1898."

The popularity of Valentine's Day grew during this time. Gifts were costly, so many valentines were homemade. In America, valentines accompanied gifts such as flowers, candy, and perfume.

By 1800, printed cards began to replace written letters due to improvements in printing technology. Ready-made cards were an easy way for people to express their thoughts and emotions in a time when direct expression of one's feelings was looked down upon. The lower postage rates also contributed to an increase in the popularity of sending a Valentine's Day greeting.

Poets or other writers would work with printers to produce the valentines. Many of these valentines were produced in booklet form, with space reserved for the sender to write a message. The cost for these works of art was around a penny.

Many countries celebrate Valentine's Day, including the United States, Canada, Mexico, the United Kingdom, France, Italy, and Australia. However, England has had by far the biggest impact on the holiday. By the 1600s, the English had a similar legend as the French,

where a girl was supposed to marry the first boy she saw on the fourteenth of February. Another English tradition was to draw slips of paper with names on them to choose your valentine for the rest of the year. Men and boys drew names of women and girls and sometimes vice versa. The couple could go to dances together, exchange gifts, or just spend the day together. If you were lucky, the person whose name you drew would be compatible, but in some cases, an older woman might be paired with a much younger man or vice versa. This really was not the most effective way of bringing lovers together, though sometimes sparks did fly!

One can only guess the true origin of Valentine's Day or the valentine card. One thing is for certain; valentines *did* catch on. According to the Greeting Card Association, an estimated 1 billion valentine cards are sent each year, making Valentine's Day the second largest card-sending holiday of the year. (An estimated 2.6 billion cards are sent for Christmas.) Women purchase approximately 85 percent of all valentines.

"Valentine Wishes—My whole affection is set upon you Please say you like me a little bit too." Marked, "Series 1080 A." Inscribed, "Dear Dick, Was awfully glad to hear from you again. You haven't moved yet—I take it. I wrote a letter and sent cards to your home. Did you get them? How are you now—we're all fine here. Love Dot."

THE BUSINESS OF CARDS

There are many different types of valentine cards, from the traditional to the far out. Many depict scenes related to the history of the valentine.

Valentines went through many changes as the years went by. Around 1840 to 1850 the new "comic" valentine was becoming more common and popular. These were not the funny style of today's valentines but rather mean-spirited remarks that were often hurtful. These "sour" types of valentines are known as "vinegar" valentines or "penny dreadfuls" and are very collectible today. Who received the vinegar cards? Several people, including those the sender was mad at or just disliked. Often they were sent anonymously to a foe, and many times they were sent postage due!

After 1840, the United States and Great Britain's mail service was greatly improved. Before this time it could take weeks to get a letter from one place to the next. When mail service improved, more people used it to send valentines.

The years from the 1840s through the 1890s were known as the "Golden Age" of valentines. A couple from England, Jonathan and Clarissa King, produced an array of beautiful valentines. It is believed that Clarissa King was the first person to put feathers on valentines. She also would take small pieces of glass and grind them into little sparkles to add to the cards. The couple's valentines became so popular that they opened a small factory employing a couple dozen workers to help them in production.

Esther A. Howland (1824-1904) from Worcester, Massachusetts, began her career working at her father's stationery shop. During the valentine season the shop would become filled with beautiful valentines from Europe. Esther thought she could make valentines just as pretty as the imported ones and for much less, so she began producing and

This gorgeous valentines says, "Valentine Greetings" on the outside, and inside the poem reads, "Take it gently off your hook, Take a careful, steady look! You will find, my Valentine That big heart you've caught is mine!" It is inscribed, "To Missie Martin From Guess Who??" Marked "Whitney Made Worcester Mass."

Many valentine cards had themes. These three feature water.

selling them at her father's shop around 1848.

In no time her work sold out and people were asking for more. She began selling her valentines to other shops in various cities. Working out of her home, Esther produced a variety of valentines with the help of hired workers. The majority ranged in price from $5 to $20, with some selling for as high as $35, a great deal of money at that time. In fact, during the 1800s $35 could buy a means of transportation such as a horse and buggy, so you can see the expenditure some consumers made for one of her works.

Esther become known as the first person to sell mass-produced or "assembly-lined" valentines in America. An enterprising woman and graduate of the Mt. Holyoke Women's Seminary, she became very wealthy. Her company expanded after the success of her valentine cards, adding Christmas and other holiday cards to the selection. Her company's sales would reach over $100,000 a year. Esther was one of the first employers to pay women a decent wage and one of the first women business owners to travel without a chaperon.

Esther developed her own style by using imported lace paper to make beautiful valentines. Some of her loveliest and earliest valentines are not signed, but collectors can recognize them by their large size and fancy, ornate style. Many of Esther Howland's later valentines are marked in the upper left-hand corner with the letter *H*. (An *H* on the right corner is from a different valentine manufacturer who produced cards about twenty years later.) After many years of producing stylish valentine cards, Esther sold her company to the Whitney Company in 1866, a major printer of children's books.

Though Esther Howland was known as one of the innovators of valentine making, other

This mechanical valentine can move back and forth. It states, "To my Valentine—Just read my heart and you will see Whose Valentine I'd love to be!"

This beautiful foldout valentine states, "To my Valentine— Loving Greetings." It is marked, "Printed in Germany" and inscribed, "To Beverly, from Martha Dunlap 1930."

women followed suit with creations of their own. Kate Greenaway (1846-1901) was one of them. Ms. Greenaway, a British artist, is well known today as an illustrator of children's books such as Robert Browning's *Pied Piper of Hamelin.* Many of her earliest works were valentines. Kate Greenaway loved to use children as the focal point of her cards. Often they depicted children giving valentines to other children. Another of her favorite subjects was the garden. The greeting card company Marcus Ward & Company produced many of her designs.

After the Whitney Company took over the Howland ventures, George C. Whitney's paper-novelty publishing company, based in Worcester, Massachusetts, became one of the most important valentine producers of the nineteenth century. Their valentines sold for many years and were cute and pretty. However, they lacked the luster of the Howland cards and, for that matter, of those made by other major valentine publishers, such as Nister and Tuck. The company focused on schoolchildren as its primary customers. Their price and designs showed that focus. From about 1910 until 1940, the majority of the Whitney cards were stand-ups, with two panels at the base that folded backward.

After the Civil War, George Whitney and his brothers Edward and Sumner organized their business and focused mainly on assembly-line production with some of the parts imported from overseas. After 1870, George Whitney took full control of the company and purchased machinery to publish more valentines as well as other greeting and holiday cards. The company closed its doors in 1942.

Whitney's largest competitor was the McLoughlin Company. Some McLoughlin valentines have a blue *H* in the upper right-

hand corner. The *H* can be confusing for collectors of Howland cards, since her cards also had an *H* in one corner. The price for collectible McLoughlin cards today, around $10 to $25, is lower than for Howland cards.

Around 1900, a popular valentine was the German foldout card with honeycomb tissue and beautiful die-cuts. Though American valentines were similar, the price of these versions was much less and they were usually not as pretty.

As Kate Greenaway did in the 1880s, many top illustrators (including Norman Rockwell,

Grace Drayton, and Francis Brundage) drew and designed valentines during the 1920s and 1930s.

As the 1900s moved onward the fascination for valentines began to wane. They were still as beautiful as ever but the cost prohibited many from purchasing them. Around this time, several things happened. First, several greeting card companies were founded, including American Greetings and Hallmark. Mass production by these companies lowered prices. Children could now afford to buy Valentine's Day cards and give them to their

This valentine states, "For My Valentine." The red heart folds over with red honeycomb tissue and may be hooked onto the back to stay open. There is also a cardboard stand on the back. Maker unknown.

friends. That tradition has not waned and today children are the main givers of Valentine's Day cards. The cards have changed greatly over the years, but their allure continues to grow. The United States and Britain lead the pack of nations celebrating Valentine's Day today. As in the earliest days of valentines, certain subjects, such as hearts, cupids, flowers, birds, and children, have remained popular. The following chapters will illustrate many of the much-loved designs and sayings from years of valentine giving.

INTERESTING FACT

Did you know that the expression "wearing your heart on your sleeve" comes from a Valentine's Day party tradition? Women would write their names on slips of paper to be drawn by men. A man would then wear a woman's name on his sleeve to claim her as his one and only—the one who would have his heart for the coming year.

CUPID'S DELIGHT

Cupid, with bow and arrow in hand, is by far one of the most popular symbols of Valentine's Day. Many of the decorations used on valentine cards and postcards are from mythology. Cupid had a magical bow and arrow, and anyone shot with his arrow would fall in love. His image was used over and over again.

There are many legends about this little winged cherub whom we have come to know as Cupid. He is the son of Venus, the Roman goddess of love. Venus was jealous of the beauty of Psyche, so she ordered Cupid to punish the mortal. Cupid fell deeply in love with her and took her as his wife. However, as a mere mortal she was forbidden to look at him.

Psyche was very happy with the arrangement until her sisters persuaded her to look at Cupid. As soon as Psyche looked at him, Cupid punished her by leaving. The lovely castle and gardens that they shared ceased to

Above: *This mechanical valentine from Germany shows a cupid and states, "To my Sweetheart." It is inscribed, "To Grandaddy From Elizabeth Mason."*

Left: *Homemade valentines are also quite nice. This one says, "Valentine greetings for Grandpa" and inside has a little poem that reads, "Whether Valentine's Day is rosy or Blue Depends entirely My Dear on you." It is signed, "Mary C., Libby, Billy & Baby."*

"To my Valentine." Signed, "Ruth from Marjorie." Maker unknown.

Gold foiling was popular on cards. This card states, "To my Valentine." It is marked, "SER. 542. No 3187." The back is marked in foreign languages.

exist. Psyche found herself alone in a field. She wandered aimlessly trying to find her true love when she came upon the temple of Venus. Venus still harbored great hatred toward Psyche and wished to destroy her. Venus gave Psyche a series of tasks to accomplish. Psyche was given a small box and was told by Venus to take it to the underworld to capture some of the beauty of Proserpina, the wife of Pluto.

She was given instructions on how to avoid the dangers of the realm of the dead and warned never to open the box under any circumstances. After a few days Psyche was overcome by temptation and opened the box. She found deadly slumber. Cupid returned to her to find her lifeless on the ground. He then gathered the deadly sleep from her body and put it back in the box. The gods, moved by Psyche's love for Cupid, made her a goddess.

Cupid, known in Latin as *Cupido* (desire), had a counterpart in Greek mythology known as Eros, god of love. He is best known as the attractive young god who falls in love with the gorgeous maiden Psyche. In the story "The Golden Ass," the Roman writer Lucius Apuleius tells of this love affair. Other stories have Cupid appearing as a mischievous little

Above: *Cupid was often depicted with hearts or flowers or both. This card says, "To My Valentine" on the cover and is postmarked February 14, 1912, Norway, Maine, on the back.*

Left: *This postcard copyrighted by F. Derbes is marked, "Valentine Series Pub. By AH: 276." It is called, "St. Valentines Messengers." It features Cupid with a sunbonneted child.*

boy who indiscriminately wounds both gods and humans with his arrows, causing them to fall deeply in love. Though Cupid is commonly represented as a naked winged infant carrying a bow and arrow, he can also be found in an array of situations, as depicted in the various postcards and greetings produced.

Greek mythology says that Eros is the son of Aphrodite. As one of the primary creators of the world, he was worshipped as the god of sexual passion and power. Eros was known to take many forms in different parts of the ancient world. Many people are not aware that Eros (Cupid) was known to have a darker, less likeable side. As a god who lived on Mt. Olympus, he engaged in many insalubrious behaviors and was thought of as a devil-

ish little fellow as well as a playful and nasty child. Eros was known to carry two types of arrows. One was golden and sharp at the point. This arrow was meant to inspire love. The other was a leaded, blunt arrow, meant to cause for the unlucky recipient depression, fear, and years of anguish.

After the mean Cupid fell in love with Psyche, his personality changed and he would be forever known as anointer of lovers. Cupid's arrows were now meant to make anyone fall madly in love, usually with the first person they laid eyes on.

Many of the cards produced from the early days of valentines until today feature Cupid. Cherubs are also quite popular on postcards and cards, but for it truly to be Cupid, he must

"My heart is drawn to you, My little steed is fine; And when I reach you, please To be my Valentine." Maker unknown.

Above: *This card states, "To My Valentine" on the cover and is marked, "5009." The back is inscribed, "February 9, 1913."*

Left: *"Valentine Greetings." Marked, "MADE IN U.S.A." with the inscription, "From Esther Fair to Caroline Routsong."*

be carrying his trusty bow and arrow. One company that used Cupid in many of its valentine designs was the International Art Publishing Company, located in New York City from the 1890s to the advent of World War I. This company was one of America's cream-of-the-crop producers of paper novelty and greeting cards. The majority of its designs were embossed and contained sparkling, colored patterns.

Ethel DeWees was another popular artist who specialized in Cupids. She worked with the A.M.P. Co., a German company that exported huge numbers of postcards to the United States in the early twentieth century. It produced many great cards, following closely the Nash Publishing Company, one of the most prolific Valentine's Day postcard manufacturers of the late 1890s. And anyone who collects Valentine's Day cards knows Raphael Tuck's versions. Their "Mischievous Cupid" series of postcards portrayed him in comical and whimsical situations.

"To my Valentine," with a heart and flowers. The back is marked, "Boston, Mass. & Germany." It is postmarked February 13, 1908. It is inscribed, "Dear George, I hope you may get many nice Valentines from a friend. Hattie Ningent."

"To my Valentine," with gold foiling. This card was postmarked February 12, 1910. German maker unknown.

One of my favorite illustrators, the great American artist Charles Dana Gibson, loved to draw Cupid in many of his designs. Gibson's cards specialized in the romantic encounters of upper-class society. In his scenes, Cupid can be found whispering in the ear of a young lady or passing an arrow from suitor to receiver.

Charles Twelvetrees, another great illustrator, who used children in many of his designs, is also well known for his use of Cupid in his works. His Series Number 75, National Cupid, for Ullman Mfg. Co., consists of twelve cute drawings showing Cupids in national costumes. Twelvetrees' use of Cupid is also seen in the many magazine illustrations he did from 1906 to the late 1930s, many of which were used as cover art.

Cupid was also a patriotic little fellow. He could be found holding or saluting a flag (these cards are rare). One London company, Birn Brothers, produced such a series from 1909 to 1910. It consisted of different scenes showing Cupid carrying, waving, or saluting the flag. Whether waving a flag or holding his bow and arrow, Cupid was a focal point in many of the early Valentine's Day postcards.

INTERESTING FACTS

The average spent on flowers for Valentine's Day has increased each year since 1998:

    1998—$26.80
    1999—$30.40
    2000—$32.10.

Where do most people shop for a valentine gift?

    Discount department stores—32 percent
    Specialty stores—18 percent
    Department stores—14 percent
    Other types of stores—14 percent
    Undetermined—10 percent
    Drugstores—7 percent
    Supermarkets—5 percent

Flowers and Cupid are often seen together on valentines. This one says, "As I fashioned this heart of for-get-me-nots, There came a thought sublime. 'Twas that these tiny bits of true blue dots, Were fit for thee 'Oh! Be my Valentine.'" This card is inscribed, "Won't you be my Valentine, dearie?" It is marked, "Cupid Valentine Series No. 1."

"A Message of Love." This pretty dove is shown on an early 1900s American post-card. Marked, "Series 444C."

ON THE WINGS
OF A DOVE

One of the legends of Valentine's Day was brought about by the way birds mate. Some say the idea of Valentine's Day originated hundreds of years ago during the mating of the birds. People in Europe saw that birds would pick their mates on or about February 14. Thus originated the idea that all species should choose their mates on this date. Since so many birds mated on February 14 it seemed a perfectly logical conclusion to pick that day as a day of "love." And so it was declared!

A white dove is said to bring good luck. Since doves and pigeons mate for life they are considered symbols of fidelity and are used on a great array of valentine greetings. Perhaps we humans can learn a few things from our fine-feathered friends. To dream of a dove is to have a promise of happiness. What is not so lovely is the fact that lovebirds are really tiny African parrots that carry disease, so there are strict import laws. You will not see lovebirds flying freely, but when they are together, it is so grand!

Chaucer wrote these words relating birds to Valentine's Day: "For this was Seynt Valentine's Day when every foul cometh ther to choose his mate."

John Donne wrote:

Hail Bishop Valentine! Whose day this is;
All the air is thy diocese,
And all the chirping choristers
And other birds are thy parishioners:
Thou marryest ever year
The lyric lark and the grave whispering dove;
The sparrow that neglects his life for love,
The household bird with the red stomarcher;
Celebrations
Thous mak'st the blackbird speed as soon,
As doth the goldfinch or the halcyon . . .
This day more cheerfully than ever shine,
This day which might inflame thyself, old Valentine!

*This beautiful mechanical valentine is German and embossed.
It is dated in pencil "1930." The front says simply, "To my
Valentine."*

This mechanical German valentine states, "To one I love." It is signed on the back, "Dorothy Bragg—1930."

This foldout valentine is marked, "Made in Germany." The front says, "To my Valentine." The German valentines are some of the most beautiful.

This foldout valentine from Germany states, "To my Valentine." It shows birds and flowers.

Let us not forget the words of the poet Michael Drayton. He wrote "To His Valentine," in which he refers to birds mating on Valentine's Day.

Each little bird this tide
Doth choose her beloved peer,
Which constantly abide
In wedlock all the year.

This large children's-style valentine shows a singing birdie. It states, "You're my Valentine! how do I know? A little birdie told me so!" Marked, "Made in U.S.A."

Another Whitney valentine. This one states, "I've found out to my great delight And I'm going to tell you, too,—You're my Valentine, yes, you are Cause my Valentine's just you." It is signed, "From Guess Who?" Marked, "Whitney Made Worcester Mass."

Hearts and birds go hand in hand on Valentine's Day cards.
Here are just a few examples. All of these postcards are from
the early 1900s.

Right: Need a little luck on Valentine's Day? This postcard says, "To My Valentine." It is marked, "EAS," was printed in Germany, and shows an unusual collection of birds, flowers, hearts, clovers, and a horseshoe for good luck.

A couple of children's valentines, ca. 1950. One is hand colored and the other has sparkles add.

INTERESTING FACTS

Avanel's Dictionary of the Saints states, "There is nothing in [the] Valentine legend to account for the custom of choosing a partner of the opposite sex and sending 'Valentines' . . . it apparently arose from an old idea that birds begin to pair on that date, but it may have a more pagan reference."

The New England Confectionery Company began making candy conversation hearts in 1902. They came in six flavors and were shaped into small hearts. Each was stamped with a little saying. They became a Valentine's Day tradition. Throughout the years, the company has produced over a hundred different sayings.

Stop!

Are you looking for a Valentine?

This beautiful foldout valentine is from Germany. It states, "Loving Greetings." The back is inscribed, "To Beverly From Mildred 1929."

"Stop! Are you looking for a Valentine? Let's go! So am I." This fun card is marked, "7540 Copyright 1921 P.F. Volland Co. Chicago."

FOR LOVERS ONLY

Valentines are often exchanged in families or among friends, but let us not forget that February 14 is a holiday particularly for romantic partners. It is celebrated around the globe. In Wales, spoons carved from wood are exchanged by lovers. In other countries, hearts with keys and keyholes are given. It is said, "The person who receives the key will be able to unlock the giver's heart!" The heart was thought by the Romans to contain the soul. The heart is the true symbol of love.

In Scotland, a lover's knot made from ribbons or paper is given to a loved one. In England, gifts include flowers, paperweights, jewels, gloves, silk stockings, garters, and handkerchiefs. Also in England, around the 1760s, it became the custom to leave a valentine love letter at the door. Little books called *Valentine's Writers* helped men to write poetry and sentimental verses.

I love thee, I love thee,
'Tis all that I can say;
It is my vision in the night,
My dreaming in the day.

Thomas Hood

This unusual valentine game sold at Skinner auction house in Boston, Massachusetts for several thousands dollars. (Courtesy of Skinner)

This fun 1950s valentine states, "To My Boy Friend—I'm looking for a valentine who's not afraid to pet. Now don't you throw me down, big boy—or you'll have me upset." Marked, "Printed in U.S.A."

The words of poet Samuel Butler are also filled with the pleasures of love:

> All love, at first, like generous wine,
> Ferments and frets until 'tis fine,
> But, when 'tis settled on the lee,
> And from th' impurer matter free,
> Becomes the richer still the older,
> And proves the pleasanter the colder.

This 1947 comical card states, "From one 'Clamor Girl' to another—We're not the prim old-fashioned gals Who'd faint when they were kissed . . . But think of the guys who made 'em swoon An' what we musta missed!" It is signed, "Thelma." Marked, "15 VH 820 Copyright MCMXLVII Rust Craft Boston, U.S.A."

They Say That Dan... In a ... Can...

I can't express the thoughts
This heart of mine would pen,
But you will understand them
I'm sure you will, so then —
I'll just say Hello!

My heart is pierced with
love for thee,
I am truly thine.
Oh, will you not
forever be
My own, sweet
Valentine?

If You'll be my SWEET
I'll be Your...

To My Valentine
Love's Offering

Valentine Greetings

Hearts are the focal point on many Valentine's Day lovers' cards.

Oh love and lovers! Since Adam and Eve, the attraction between man to woman has been embedded in us, body and soul. Let me share some interesting facts about lovers you may not know.

INTERESTING FACTS

If you are a woman looking for love, you have the advantage in Virginia and Colorado. Women may want to set out for Crowley County, Colorado, where there are 205.4 men to every 100 women! Now that is what I call a woman's paradise.

The number of marriages performed in Nevada during 2000 was 144,300. So many couples married in the Silver State that it ranked fourth nationally in weddings, even though in total population it ranked thirty-fifth, according to the 2000 census. Neighboring California, with more than sixteen times as many residents, registered only about 50,000 more marriages.

Did you know that 52 percent of women and 56 percent of men in America who were fifteen and over married in 2000? These percentages have fallen from 60 percent and 65 percent, respectively, in 1970. Also, it appears that men like younger women. Only 12 percent of wives were two or more years older than their husbands in 2000. (Source: U.S. Census.)

More than 35 million heart-shaped boxes of candy and chocolate are sold each year for Valentine's Day. According to a survey by the Chocolate Manufacturers Association, 50 percent of women will more than likely give a gift of chocolate to the men in their lives for Valentine's Day.

Valentine's Day is known as the "last-minute holiday." More than 75 percent of all purchases are made the week before the holiday!

Teachers receive the most valentines, followed by children, mothers, wives, and then sweethearts.

Silhouettes are also quite popular for Valentine's Day cards. These two pictures state, "Valentine Greetings—They tumble right over each other, Best wishes happy and gay; They jostle and crowd one another To greet you on Valentine's Day" and "Valentine Thoughts Of You—My happiest and fondest thoughts Are sent to you to say, They greet you as a Valentine On this very special day."

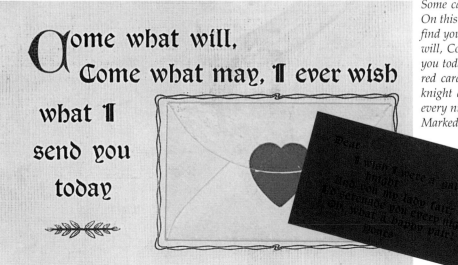

Some cards make you work for your valentine. On this one you must open the small envelope to find your card. The postcard reads, "Come what will, Come what may, I ever wish what I send you today." Inside the small envelope a separate red card reads, "Dear, I wish I were a gallant knight and you my lady fair; I'd serenade you every night, Oh, what a happy pair! Yours . . ." Marked, "W. M. Beach Co., Roxbury, Mass."

Couples on valentines show the romantic side of February 14.
Here are three examples, all ca. 1920.

This colorful embossed valentine reads, "To my Valentine."
The back is marked, "Made in Germany, 803." It is postmarked February 15, 1910.

Some people like to give more humorous cards, like these two.
One says, "Seeing you again . . . Valentine it's been so wonderful." The other says, "Stop going around in circles, ya
square—A valentine to a big wheel."

Larger cards like these are more rare than the smaller versions. Clockwise from bottom: A 1950s mechanical bellhop valentine is marked, "A-MERI-CARD Made in U.S.A. 0-4590." Next is another 1950s card showing a pretty woman. "Always a Bridesmaid but never a Bride. Can't you take a hint?" This card is marked, "Carrington Co., Chicago, Ill." And last is an early 1900s mechanical valentine that reads, "Be my Valentine. I've a notion, I'm in motion." Maker unknown.

Mothers enjoy receiving valentines too. This one reads, "With Love to Mother on Valentine's Day—A greeting of love, holding happiest thoughts And memories dear to recall Of the sweetest; the dearest the finest, the best Most lovable Mother of all!" Marked, "Made in U S A."

A ROSE FOR YOUR THOUGHTS

Roses symbolize many things: peace, war, love, forgiveness. A gift of roses means, "I love you passionately."

What's in a name? That which we call a rose
By any other name would smell as sweet;
So Romeo would, were he not Romeo called.

William Shakespeare

This large embossed valentine was given as a birthday gift. It is inscribed, "A Happy Birthday from Lillian."

This darling child in the garden is growing lots of Cupids! The card reads, "I like a maid, hope she likes me; We're not sweethearts, may never be She's quite the nicest girl I know, So I send this valentine just to tell her so." Marked, "Whitney Made Worcester Mass."

"Fond Rememberance." This card with several blue flowers is dated 1909.

Flowers have been around since the beginning of time. They have been given as gifts for nearly as long. It is said that gifts of flowers on February 14 became popular when one of Henry IV's daughters received a bouquet from her chosen valentine. What are the meanings of the different kinds? What is the best flower to give to a loved one?

Flowers have always been a major theme in valentine cards and postcards. Certain flowers are used more frequently, such as the rose or lily. Since flowers and Valentine's Day go hand in hand, we need to explore the meanings and legends of some of the most often given flowers as well as the reason their images were used on greeting cards.

> *O, my luve's like a red red rose*
> *That's newly sprung in June.*
> *O my luve's like a melodie*
> *That's sweetly played in tune.*
>
> Robert Burns

"Wheresoever fate may take us And we sometimes drift apart, There is still a little corner For you always in my heart." Marked, "29." Dated in pencil August 20, 1909.

LOVE'S OFFERING.

Many varieties of flowers are used on valentines. These postcards show just a few. As you can see, they are the focal point of the card. All three are embossed and were produced in the early 1900s.

My Heart's Own Valentine.

THE ROSE

There are many legends as to how certain flowers came into existence. For instance, it is thought that the red rose was initially white. From Persia, Allah chose a white rose to be the Queen of the Flowers. One night, Allah, in the form of a nightingale, flew toward the rose, attracted to its beautiful fragrance. The thorns of the flower stabbed Allah and his blood dyed it red.

The rose is also an ancient symbol for a goddess. In the East, it was called the "Flower of the Goddess." In the West, the white rose was the sign for a virgin, while the red rose showed a goddess in her complete sexual maturity. Roses are considered sacred to Aphrodite, the Greek goddess of love. In Christianity, the Virgin Mary has been called "Queen of the Rose Garden," "Mystic Rose," and "Rose of Heavens." Even the fairy tales use the rose as a symbol, including "Briar Rose" and "Snow White."

The meaning of the rose's color has changed slightly over time.

Older Meanings

White roses mean true love.
Red roses mean passion.
Yellow roses mean friendship.
Black roses mean farewell.

Modern Meanings

White roses mean purity of the mind, innocence, charm, or unity.
Red roses mean love, desire, or unity.
Yellow roses mean friendship.
Pink roses mean friendship, romance, or perfect happiness.
Rosebuds mean beauty and youth.
Black roses mean hate and death.

This early 1950s card states, "A Valentine Wish—A Valentine wish From a heart sincere, Be my love now And forever, dear." Marked, "Doubl-glo, L1731-1 Made in U. S. A."

Only a Greeting
with
Sincere
Love

My devoted Heart
is thine,
Thee I Love
My Valentine

Children with flowers were a popular theme on valentines. These three are embossed and from the early 1900s. None is marked.

Love's Reminder.

CARING FOR YOUR ROSES

An estimated 103 million roses were sold for Valentine's Day 2001. Did you know that men make 70 percent of flower purchases on Valentine's Day? Of the cut flowers purchased, 46 percent are roses, 36 percent mixed flowers, 11 percent carnations, and 7 percent other single flower types. Of roses purchased, 65 percent are red, 9 percent mixed, 8 percent pink, 6 percent peach/salmon, 5 percent yellow, 4 percent white, and 3 percent other.

Once you have the roses, here is the best way to keep them fresh.

1. Remove any torn leaves. Thorns can be removed without harm to the flower.

2. Re-cut the stems under running water before arranging. If you are not able to put the flowers in water right away, then store them in the refrigerator.

3. Remove any leaves that would be below the water surface.

4. Use room-temperature water and change the water daily.

5. Floral preservative can be added to the water at every change. A quarter teaspoon (per large vase) of bleach can be added if a floral preservative is not available.

6. Keep flowers away from bright sunlight.

7. At night move the flowers to the coolest part of the house.

The beautiful red, pink or ivory perennial that blooms in the spring can be grown in containers in partial shade. After the bloom, when the foliage turns yellow, cut the top off each stem.

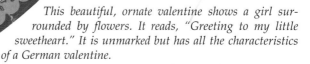

This beautiful, ornate valentine shows a girl surrounded by flowers. It reads, "Greeting to my little sweetheart." It is unmarked but has all the characteristics of a German valentine.

A Valentine Message

I have to join two
hearts in one,
And wish this tender
task were done.

805

To my Valentine.

Hearts and flowers make for an eye-catching valentine. Here are four
examples dating from the early 1900s to the 1950s.

OTHER FLOWERS

Let us look at some other flowers and leaves, their legends, and their meanings.

Bachelor Button: Celibacy. According to Greek legend, Flora, the goddess of flowers, turned her devotee, Kyanus, into this flower at his death.

Bayleaf: Hope.

Begonia: A fanciful nature.

Bleeding Heart: Hopeless but not heartless.

Carnation, red: Admiration.

Carnation, white: Pure and ardent love.

Chrysanthemum, red: I love you.

Chrysanthemum, white: Truth.

Daffodil: Regard.

Daisy: Innocence, gentleness. According to Greek legend, a wood nymph was seen by the god of spring. She was changed into a daisy when she became frightened.

Forget-Me-Not: True love.

Gardenia: I secretly love you.

Gladiolus: You pierce my heart. Do not give white gladiolus on Valentine's Day. They are for funerals. White and yellow flowers are funeral flowers in some countries.

Hibiscus: Delicate beauty.

Jasmine, white: Amiability.

Jasmine, yellow: Modesty.

Larkspur: An open heart.

Lily of the Valley: Let us make up.

Pansy: Thoughtful recollection.

Primrose: Young love.

Sweet William: You are gallant and suave.

Tulips: We are perfect lovers.

Verbena: You may get your wish.

Violet: I return your love. Also modesty and simplicity.

The legends of the flowers and plants are plentiful. Here are but a few.

According to Greek legend, Aphrodite turned beautiful women blue and shrunk them into violets when Cupid refused to say that she was more beautiful.

St. Valentine's garden was filled with beautiful flowers and he gave them freely to children. When he was jailed the children missed him and threw him bouquets of flowers through the prison bars.

A pink almond tree planted at St. Valentine's gravesite burst into bloom immediately as a symbol of everlasting love.

In Germany, women would plant onions in pots and then give each a man's name. They would then place the pots near the fireplace. The first onion to sprout would be the husband-to-be!

To my true Love

PHILADELPHIA
FEB 12
9 30A
18 08
PA.

RD STATION

THE ADDRESS TO BE WRITTEN
ON THIS SIDE.

PRINTED IN GERMANY

Miss Eemma Kiesacker
Greencastle
Franklin Co
Penna

INTERESTING FACTS

The wholesale value of domestically produced cut flowers in 2000 was $427 million. California was the leading producer in the U.S., alone accounting for two-thirds of this amount ($286 million).

The wholesale value of domestically produced roses in 2000 was $69 million. Roses generated the highest receipts of any type of cut flower, followed by lilies ($59 million).

In 1999, the number of florists nationwide was 24,798. These businesses employed 121,783 people. (Source for the above: U.S. Department of Agriculture.)

The value of United States imports of cut flowers from Colombia between January and October 2001 was $61 million. Colombia was the leading foreign supplier of cut flowers for the United States. (Source: U.S. Census.)

*There are few, dear
Just like you, dear
There are none I hold your equal
So be true, dear
Let me woo, dear
Till my tale will bring its sequal.*

Many cards were mailed without a return address, leaving the recipient to wonder whom their secret valentine might be. Here are two examples of early 1900s postcards with flowers, both without a return address.

There are many folks
In the world, it's true ~ ~

But to me there's NO ONE
Just like you!

From Guess who??

A *Valentine*
Thought

To You

Valentines
can be elaborate,
with fuzzy hearts or cut-out
covers. The top card states, "A Valentine
Thought—There are many folks In the world, it's
true—But to me there's NO ONE Just like you!" It is
signed, "From Guess Who???" The bottom card reads,
"Valentine Greetings To You—One of the pleasures of
Valentine's Day Is this chance to say anew, Just how
grand it is to know someone As wonderful as you."

One of the pleasures of Valentine's Day
Is this chance to say anew.

Just how grand it is to know someone
As wonderful as you.

A VALENTINE MESSAGE

This is just a word of greeting,
On a postal card, you see.
Just a whispered, "I remember!"
Will you send the same to me?

"A Valentine Message—This is just a word of greeting, On a postal card, you see. Just a whispered, "I remember!" Will you send the same to me?" Inscribed, "From Ralph S To Miss Klase." Marked, "J.P., N.Y."

This unusual mechanical valentine shows different scenes when you turn the circle. It states, "I'll catch-up to you—my Love."

This pretty embossed card states, "To My Sweet Love From . . ."
Marked, "A. Hall."

Valentine
Greetings
Come fly with me,
Your hand in mine
And you shall be
My Valentine.

This foldout valentine was produced in Germany. It states,
"Valentine Greetings—Come fly with me, Your hand in mine
And you shall be My Valentine." Signed on the back in pen-
cil, "1930 To Beverly from Masy."

How precious are these mechanical children's valentines from the early 1900s! Clockwise from top left: "See what? little Bo peeps' sheep has brought for you." Marked, "Made in U.S.A." Then, "My Sweetheart, I'm in the MARKET for You." Marked, "Made in Germany" and signed, "1935—From William Camper To Rena Elliot." Lastly, "I'll sail all the seas after you my Valentine." Marked, "Printed in Germany."

GIRLS WILL BE GIRLS
AND BOYS WILL BE BOYS!

Children have become the givers of many of the valentines today. Little girls scribble love messages to their sweeties and pass them along. In the British Isles, children get candy or money for singing special carols on Valentine's Day. This custom started in the 1700s. At that time, children dressed up as adults on Valentine's Day and went singing from home to home. One verse they sang was:

Good morning to you, Valentine;
Curl your locks as I do mine—
Two before and three behind.
Good morning to you, Valentine.

This large valentine has a foldout design. It states, "You see it's written in my heart you're my Valentine." Marked, "Made in Germany."

This fun mechanical valentine reveals a young couple kissing. It states, "If you want me for a fellow Just try this in a Yellow." Marked, "Carrington Co. Chicago, Ill. 802." Dated 1926.

Other traditions involve Valentine's Day parties. In England and France in the seventeenth and eighteenth centuries, wealthy people threw such parties. In Victorian times children threw parties as well. They played games, ate heart-shaped sweets and cookies, and gave each other valentines and gifts. This tradition continues today.

One popular game that children play consists of thinking of several boys or girls they might marry and then twisting the stem of an apple while reciting the names until the stem comes off. The person they will marry is the one whose name they were reciting when the stem fell off.

What of the games that determine how many children you will have? Try this to see! Pick a dandelion that has gone to seed. Take a deep breath and blow the seeds with all your might into the wind. Now count the seeds that remain on the stem. That is how many children you will have!

Here is another way to see how many children you may have. Cut an apple in half and count the seeds inside. That is how many children you will have!

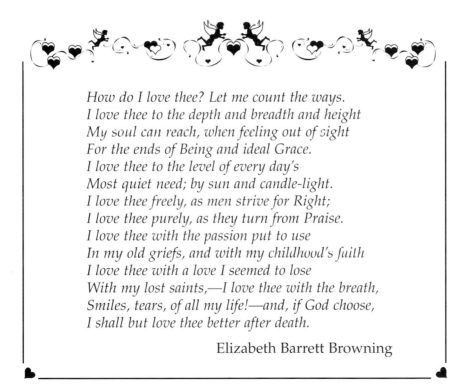

How do I love thee? Let me count the ways.
I love thee to the depth and breadth and height
My soul can reach, when feeling out of sight
For the ends of Being and ideal Grace.
I love thee to the level of every day's
Most quiet need; by sun and candle-light.
I love thee freely, as men strive for Right;
I love thee purely, as they turn from Praise.
I love thee with the passion put to use
In my old griefs, and with my childhood's faith
I love thee with a love I seemed to lose
With my lost saints,—I love thee with the breath,
Smiles, tears, of all my life!—and, if God choose,
I shall but love thee better after death.

Elizabeth Barrett Browning

JUST BURSTING TO ASK YOU TO BE MY VALENTINE

I CAN KEEP A SECRET SO BE MY VALENTINE

I'LL NEVER FOR-GET YOU MY VALENTINE

I'LL SAY IT WITH MUSIC I WANT YOU FOR MY VALENTINE

HOW "A-BOOT" IT? DO YOU

I'M NOT TRYING TO STRING YOU MY VALENTINE

Small valentines were given out to class-mates. Here are some examples of 1930s cards for school.

More examples of classroom valentine cards are these inexpensive ones from the 1930s.

INTERESTING FACTS

Children love candy and enjoy giving and receiving it on Valentine's Day. Check out these fun valentine facts!

The value of United States imports of chocolate and other foods containing cocoa from Canada, the leading country of origin for such imports, between January and October 2001 was $363 million.

The number of establishments in Pennsylvania producing chocolate and cocoa products in 1999 was 112, leading the nation in chocolate making.

Candy sales are sweet for many, especially the sellers. Just look at the sales figures for Valentine's Day candies over the last few years, in millions of dollars.

1995	1996	1997	1998	1999	2000	2001	2002*
$782	$838	$955	$1,033	$1,011	$1,059	$1,055	$1,090

*Projected
(Source: National Confectioners Association.)

Large valentines like these are rare for a child's card. The first reads, "I Love You—I Love You—You're just as nice as you can be As almost anyone can see That's why I send this little line To say, 'Please Be My Valentine!'" The other large valentine shows a little boy on a train. Unmarked.

Many children's valentines show them busy at work or play, as these cards depict.

This valentine came with a lollipop that slid through the opening. It is marked, "Mfd. By E. Rosen Company Providence, R. I."

I'm signalling you to stop
To look and listen, too,
So that when you get
this pop
You'll know that I love you.

This small card can be opened from either side. The inside reads, "Presume I always had a heart Although I never knew I had one till the moment when I first laid eyes on you."

This beautiful card was produced by Whitney. It opens up to say, "No eye so bright, no foot so light, No heart so tender and true, As those of a little girl Who can set my heart a-twirl And that little Girl is YOU."

These fun little 1950s valentine cards were sold in assortment boxes.

This 1950s mechanical, stand-up valentine would look very nice on a teacher's desk. It reads, "Bored of Education? Not if you're the 'Subject' Valentine!" A tab on the back moves the boy's head away from the book to reveal that the girl has written the word "Love" with chalk. Marked, "A-MERI-CARD Made in U.S.A. 0-197."

TEACHER'S PET

In the United States in 2001, over one billion valentines were delivered. So, you may ask, who is receiving all these cards? The most popular receivers of valentine cards today are mothers, wives, sweethearts, children, and, yes, teachers. Since Valentine's Day is so popular in schools today, you will see an array of valentines for the adult in the classroom, the teacher. Many of the teacher cards are sweet, with very few portraying a mean instructor. After all, wouldn't you want to make your teacher happy?

Valentine's Day in the classroom has grown into an exciting event, with crafts and parties abounding. Here are a few things you can do!

CRAFTS TO MAKE

Craft Recipe No. 1
Heart-Shaped Soap

This is fun to make and give as a gift, but please do not try to eat it!

Begin with a plastic heart-shaped mold (cupcake molds work best). Do not use metal molds. Then you will need a bar of glycerin soap in a color you like. Reds, pinks, and yellows are favorites.

Carefully cut the bar of soap with a knife into pieces that will fit into the heart mold. Place the mold on a microwave-safe dish. Microwave on low for about 3 minutes, until the soap is melted into liquid form. Remove from the microwave and allow to harden. Remove from mold and you have your heart-shaped soap! This is a quick and easy gift idea.

Craft Recipe No. 2
Valentine's Day Pasta Pictures

They say a picture is worth a thousand words.

Dye different shapes pasta with red food coloring. Do this by putting the uncooked pasta in cold water with the food coloring. Leave the pasta in only a few seconds, just enough to let the water cover the noodle. Then set the pasta out on wax paper and let dry. After the pasta is completely dry, glue, on a big piece of heavy, red construction paper, the pasta in the shape of hearts and words, such as:

"I Love You"
"Be Mine"
"Yours Always"

A variation on this is to use red-hot cinnamon candies to make the pictures and words.

This mechanical card is school related but could have been given to any little girl in class. Marked, "Made in U.S.A."

Craft Recipe No. 3
Heart-Shaped Pins or Brooches

Here is another fun gift idea to make but not to eat.

1 cup flour
1 cup warm water
2 tsp. cream of tartar
1 tsp. oil
1 tsp. salt
Red food coloring
Safety pins

In a saucepan, mix together the flour, water, cream of tartar, oil, and salt. Stir over medium heat for a few minutes until smooth, adding food coloring at the end. Remove from the pan. When cool enough to handle, knead until well blended. Shape into hearts and press safety pins into the backs of the hearts before they harden. Be sure that the opening/closing part of each pin is not pressed into the heart or it will not move properly when the heart is dry.

This chalkboard scene states, "I know you like a book my Valentine." It is marked,"Made in U.S.A." and inscribed, "From Nillian To Rena."

Most teacher's valentines are larger than children's, but here are a few of the smaller versions to see.

Craft Recipe No. 4
Valentine's Day Bookmark

Cut a 5-inch by 2-inch strip from red construction paper. Then cut white and pink heart shapes ranging from about one-half inch to just less than 2 inches wide. Glue the hearts onto the bookmark. Punch a small hole in the center of the bookmark about one-half inch from the top and put a red or pink ribbon through the hole, then tie near the hole, leaving some ribbon to trail out of the bookmark! That is it—quick and fun!

Craft Recipe No. 5
A Pot of Kisses

Take a glass jar and decorate it by painting little red hearts on it. You could also add heart-shaped stickers or glue on hearts or little sayings like "I Love You." Fill the jar with Hershey's Kisses. Drop in red hots for added color. Finish off with a red bow or ribbon on the top of the jar.

This teacher's valentine states, "To My Teacher On Valentine's Day—Greetings on Valentine's Day to the nicest person I know—My Teacher!"

Craft Recipe No. 6
Magical Carnations

Take half a dozen white carnations. Cut off the ends and place in a vase of warm water. Place a few drops of red food dye or food coloring in the vase and watch the magic begin! Slowly your white carnations will turn Valentine's Day red.

Craft Recipe No. 7
Hearts from the Hands

Children love to play with finger paints. Make some white, red, and pink paint and give each child white construction paper. See what great valentines they can create! Here is the recipe for finger paint.

$1/2$ cup cornstarch
4 cups cold water
Red food coloring

Mix cornstarch and water in saucepan. Boil 3-5 minutes until mixture thickens. Cool, then pour into three separate jars. To one jar, add enough red food coloring to make red paint. To another jar, add a little red food coloring to make pink paint. Leave the last jar of paint white.

Most teacher cards do not say, "I Love You" but this card does. The inside reads, "You are everything I like the best You are all that's kind and true I guess that is the reason why I think so much of you." Marked, "Carrington Co. Chicago, Ill." Signed, "Helbert."

Craft Recipe No. 8
Valentine Placemats

Collect old valentines. Glue decoratively onto light cardboard or construction paper that is the size of a placemat. To make your creation last, cover the collage with clear contact paper, sealing the placemat. Be sure to have your child date and sign it. These make wonderful gifts for parents and grandparents.

Teacher's valentines could come from a boy or a girl in the class. These two were made in the U.S.A. and numbered 150A and 150D.

GAMES TO PLAY

Game No. 1
Can You Guess?

Take several jars and fill them with assorted valentine candies. Use one type per jar. Fill one with Hershey's Kisses, one with red hots, one with peppermint candies, and so on. Count each piece as you put it in the jar. Leave a piece of paper and a pencil next to each jar. Have the kids list their names on the papers with their guesses of how many candies are in the jars. The one who is closest to the correct number wins that jar of candy or a prize.

Game No. 2
Candy Toss

Take a piece of red construction paper and draw three concentric circles in the middle, like a bull's-eye. Color each circle a different color, then write in different point values for each. Have each child throw a candy at the circles. Give them three throws each. When a child hits a circle, he gets that circle's number of points. Add up the points each child has accumulated and give prizes for the most points. M&Ms or jellybeans work well to toss.

Game No. 3
Valentine's Day Candy Treasure Hunt

Hide candy bars (the miniature kind works best) around the room and have the children find them! Pick one candy to hide as the grand prize (a large candy bar will do). Whoever finds the big prize can choose whichever prize he wants. Of course, other children can win smaller prizes too! Have prizes for the child who finds the most candy and the least candy. Make sure everyone gets at least something, even if it is only a piece of the candy! Decorate a box with Valentine's Day decorations and let the winners draw a prize out of the box.

This pretty foldout from the 1950s was an expensive card at the time. It states, "My Valentine for You—for Teacher—will you be mine? You know I like you very much, No reason you should doubt it—I thought there might be something You could do about it—Like Being My Valentine."

These two 1950s valentines use flowers as their main theme.

INTERESTING FACT

In 2000, there were 13.3 million people aged twenty-five to thirty-four who had never been married. This number represented 35 percent of the age group. The total of never-been-marrieds in the thirty-five to forty-four age bracket was 6.9 million, or 15 percent.

From St. Valentine

To my Valentine
I'm wearing blue
forget-me-nots
Within this heart of mine,
Because you see, I like
you lots,
My Pretty Valentine!

Postcards were also popular gifts to teachers on Valentine's Day. Clockwise from top left: A Tuck's postcard from 1914, a U.S.A.-made postcard with a little boy holding a heart, and another U.S.A.-made postcard with children skating from 1913.

Valentine Greetings

vant to shkate
thru life mit
you, dear von
efer undt efer.

8000

To My Valentine

🖤

A case full of love I've brought you here

From some one to whom you are very dear;

Who somebody is I may not say;

I think you will guess though right away.

To my Valentine

Right under my hands

I've a feeling so queer...

I declare **I** dont know what to do

For **I**'m sure if **I** took my

Hands away now

My heart would fly straight off to you!

These two doll postcards would make perfect valentines for any teacher or little girl. The first is a photograph of a doll with this poem: "To My Valentine—A case full of love I've brought you here From some one to whom you are very dear; Who somebody is I may not say; I think you will guess though right away." It is marked, "AR-6—copyright 1908. Helen L. McCarthy." The second is a Tuck's postcard dated 1912.

A Valentine Message

I've asked you once, I'll ask you twice
I'll ask you seven times seven;
For if you'll be my Valentine,
This earth will be my Heaven.

Dear Valentine
Why be lonesome
Why dontcha be
my little
OWNSOME?

Clarice

Bobby and
Wayne.

Crafts are fun to do in pairs! Here are some charming valentines with a duo of children.

*This foldout valentine was made in the U.S.A. It states,
"We're up above the world so high, Dear Valentine, Just you
and I."*

RECIPES FOR LOVE

They say that the way to a man's heart is through his stomach! Show him how much you love him with these fun and tasty recipes. Many of the recipes presented here have been passed down from generation to generation. Some are new ones that my children and I "invented." All are worthy of taking an afternoon off to prepare for yourself or that special someone.

Recipe No. 1
Candied Rose Petals

   ¾ cup rose petals
   ¾ cup water
   1 cup sugar
   Red food coloring
   Ice cubes
   Powdered sugar

Rinse rose petals and place on a towel to dry. Then trim around the rose petals, discarding the ends.

Combine water and sugar in a pan. If you want to make the color of the rose petals more vibrant, add 1 or 2 drops red food coloring to the mixture in the pan. Boil about 5 minutes until syrupy. Pour syrup into a bowl of ice cubes.

When syrup begins to crystallize, hold petals with tweezers and dip. Hold for a moment to set, then lay on wax paper and dust with powdered sugar.

Recipe No. 2
Strawberry Ice Cream Punch

This gives a great look to a party table.
   2 ltr. lemon-lime soda
   1 qt. strawberry ice cream
   Fresh strawberries

Pour chilled soda into a punch bowl. Add ice cream, leaving it in one "whole" piece in the middle. Cut a few strawberries in half and trim each in the shape of a heart. Drop into soda. (Raspberries can be substituted if any guest has allergies to strawberries.)

This fun 1940s valentine is two-sided. The front says, "Can't I be your popsy-wop? To my Valentine." The flip side says, "Don't keep me in suspense any longer" and shows the fellow hanging from a tree limb by his suspenders.

Comical valentines were popular. Here are two examples.

Recipe No. 3
Valentine's Day Chocolate Cheesecake

This is from my mother's recipe file—a family favorite.

    2 cups crushed vanilla wafers
    1 cup ground toasted almonds
    ½ cup melted butter
    ½ cup sugar
    12-14 oz. chocolate chips
      (milk chocolate are best)
    ½ cup milk
    1 env. unflavored gelatin
    ½ cup sour cream
    3 8-oz. pkg. cream cheese, softened
    ½ tsp. almond extract
    ½ cup whipped heavy cream
    Whipped cream and chocolate shavings
      (optional)

In a large bowl, combine vanilla wafer crumbs, almonds, butter, and sugar; mix together well. Pat firmly into 9-inch spring-form pan. Be sure to cover bottom and about 2 to 2½ inches up the sides. Now set this aside.

Melt the chocolate chips over hot water; do not boil. Stir until melted and smooth.

Put milk in saucepan and sprinkle gelatin over the top. Cook over low heat, stirring constantly until gelatin dissolves. Be careful not to burn it. Set aside for now.

In another large bowl, mix sour cream, cream cheese, and melted chocolate chips; beat until fluffy. Beat in gelatin mixture and almond extract. Fold in whipped cream. Pour mixture into prepared pan and chill until firm (usually takes 2½ to 3 hours).

To separate cake from pan, run a warm butter knife around the edge, then spring open the pan. Remove cake and garnish with whipped cream and chocolate shavings, if desired. Yum!

Recipe No. 4
Valentine's Day Strawberry Angel Fluff

I *love* this one—so quick and easy.

    1 large pkg. frozen whipped topping
    1 pkg. frozen strawberries
    1 angel-food cake
    1 large pkg. Strawberry Jell-O
    2 cups boiling water
    2 cups cold water
    Fresh strawberries
    Whipped topping

Thaw out whipped topping and strawberries. Tear the cake into bite-size pieces and scatter over bottom of a 10-inch by 13-inch sheet-cake pan.

Dissolve Jell-O in the boiling water and then add the cold water. Put in refrigerator and allow to jell slightly.

Fold the thawed strawberries and whipped topping into the Jell-O. Pour over cake and refrigerate until set. Decorate with fresh strawberries and whipped topping.

Here's an unusual valentine, sold in a leap year. It could really be given any time of the year. It reads, "Remember Girlie, it's leap year! Once in four years So they say Things will come A maiden's way ... And so since custom says you can, Go right out and GET YOUR MAN!" Marked, "15 VH 816 copyright MCMXLVII Rust Craft Boston, U. S. A."

To My Valentine

Please Take A Little Interest

I'm Just Like Money In The Bank, And That's No Idle Jest. Why Am I Like A Bank Account? Don't I Draw Interest?

PRINTED IN U.S.A.

This cartoon-style valentine states, "To my Valentine—Please take a little interest—I'm just like money in the bank, and that's no idle jest. Why am I like a bank account? Don't I draw interest?" Marked, "Printed in U.S.A."

Sample of our
VALENTINE MECHANICALS
No. 421.   Six designs.
With movable heads. Special value.
Retail at 2¢ each with envelope.
OUR SPECIAL PRICE IS
25c per 25, or $1.00 per 100, postpaid.
Including envelopes to match.
NYCE MFG. CO.,   VERNFIELD, PA.

BOX OFFER NO. 37 —— This is one of 100 assorted Valentine Folders, Mechanicals, Cut-Outs and Pull-Outs, all with envelopes to match, retailing at 2c each, sent postpaid for $1.00.

This old envelope tells all about valentine mechanicals. For a penny apiece you could get quite a selection!

Recipe No. 5
Valentine's Day Red Hot Ice Cubes

Put cinnamon red hots and water in an ice tray. Put in as many red hots as you can fit and still have them under the water. Let them freeze. Serve the cubes in a glass of juice or soda, or put a bunch in a punch bowl.

Recipe No. 6
Red Hot Valentine's Day Salad

6 oz. (2 pkg.) Cherry or Strawberry Jell-O
4 oz. cinnamon red hots
3 cups boiling water
20 oz. crushed undrained pineapple chunks
2 cups applesauce

Dissolve Jell-O and cinnamon red hots in the boiling water. Set aside and let cool to room temperature. When cooled, add pineapple pieces and applesauce. Pour into well-oiled 8-cup mold. Chill before serving.

 INTERESTING FACTS

Valentine's Day is the fourth largest holiday for candy sales—$1.055 billion in 2001. Halloween ranked number one with $1.983 billion, followed by Easter with $1.856 billion and the winter holidays with $1.431 billion.

Did you know that the per-capita consumption of candy by Americans in 2000 was twenty-five pounds? Yes, that is per person!

There were 3,885 confectionary and nut stores in the United States in 1999.

In England, women eat hard-boiled eggs with salt and put green leaves under their pillows on Valentine's Day in hopes of dreaming of their intended husbands. Also in England, special valentine's buns are prepared, baked with raisins, caraway seeds, and plum filling.

A collection of small children's valentines makes a great display. See how cute they look when arranged together.

These 1950s valentines show a musical theme. Others show sports themes, as in the next set.

JUST A LINE
FOR MY VALENTINE

BROKEN HEARTS
MENDED

*Hearts always make nice theme
cards. Display ones like these on a
piece of black cardboard to offset the color.*

THIS HEART WILL TELL YOU
SWEETHEART MINE
I'LL ALWAYS BE YOUR
VALENTINE

This embossed, gold-foil postcard states, "This heart will tell you sweetheart mine I'll always be your Valentine." The back is inscribed, "To Mother and Daddy With much love, from Mary C., Libby, Billy and Baby."

HOW DO I LOVE THEE?
LET ME COUNT THE WAYS

There are many ways to say, "I love you!" Here are just a few.

American Sign Language:
  (signed with right hand):

Afrikaans: Ek is life vir jou!

Amharic: Afekrishalehou!

Arabic: Ohiboke (male or female); Nohiboka (female to male or male to male)

Bosnian: Volim te!

Bulgarian: Obicham te!

Creole: Mi aime jou!

Czech: Miluji te!

Danish: Jeg elsker dig!

English: I love you!

Filipino: Iniibig kita!

French: Je t'aime!

German: Ich liebe dich!

Greek: S'ayapo!

Hawaiian: Aloha wau ia 'oe!

Hebrew: Anee ohev otakh (male to female); Anee ohevet otkha (female to male); Anee ohev otkha (male to male); Anee ohevet otakh (female to female)

Hungarian: Szeretlek!

Indonesian: Saya cinta padamu!

Irish: t'a gr'a agam dhuit!

Italian: Ti amo!

Japanese: Kimi o ai shiteru!

Korean: Dangsinul saranghee yo!

Latin: Te amo!

Norwegian: Jeg elsker deg!

Polish: Kocham ciebie!

Portuguese: Eu te amo!

Romanian: Te iubesc!

Russian: Ya tyebya lyublyu!

Spanish: Te amo!

Swedish: Jag älskar dig!

Thai: Phom rug khun (male); Chan rug khun (female)

Turkish: Seni seviyorum!

Ukrainian: Ya tebe kokhayu!

Vietnamese: Anh yeu em (male to female); Em yeu an (female to male)

*This large lithograph of a little Cupid watering hearts is so pre-
cious! Lots of "I Love You's" are popping up everywhere.*

INTERESTING FACTS

In 1993, Christie's of London devoted an entire auction to valentines. They sold 1,500 cards in 313 lots for $35,000.

Pook & Pook Inc. Auction of Americana in Pennsylvania sold a single hand-painted, intricately cut paper valentine made in the 1800s for $38,500.

In Japan, girls give special candies to the boys in their classrooms who have no sweethearts to send them gifts.

This companion piece is just as precious as its mate. This Cupid picks the hearts and puts them in a basket. Both cards are marked, "Litho in U.S.A."

Cat postcards for Valentine's Day are rare. This one states, "My heart is yours fur-ever Valentine." It is marked, "Whitney Made Worcester Mass. Made in U.S.A."

AH, MY PET

According to research conducted by Hartz, 3 percent of pet owners give gifts to their pets for Valentine's Day (compared to nearly 50 percent for Christmas or Hanukkah). But remember, if you are an animal lover, never give your dog chocolate. It's tasty to you but can be toxic to canines!

There is very little written about Valentine's Day and pets. Yet there is a great variety of Valentine's Day cards produced with animals as the primary theme. Dogs and cats are the animals used most often. Bunnies come in next, followed by an array of animals from donkeys to monkeys. Though this chapter is small in words, it is great in examples and images. I hope you enjoy them.

This rare lithographed valentine came complete with a chain for the doggy. It states, "I love you Dog-on well." It was printed in Germany.

These classroom-style valentine cards feature pets and simple greetings on the front, with short poems inside.

INTERESTING FACTS

In Denmark, young people exchange pressed snowdrops and original poems. A humorous message called a *Gaekkebrev* can be sent. It is signed with a line of dots, one for each letter in the sender's name. If the recipient guesses who the sender is, the sender should receive a candy egg at Easter.

The Roman Catholic Church's official encyclopedia of saints lists seventeen Valentines, which include ones from France, Spain, Italy, and Germany. However, the church takes a neutral stance, designating no patron saint of lovers.

This great mechanical valentine will keep you hopping! It states, "Excuse me for 'buttin'' in—but—it's gonna get my 'goat' if you won't be my valentine!"

Grandmas like to get Valentine's Day cards too! This one states, "For my grandmother with love—You'd make a perfect Valentine! Grandmother, will you Please be mine?" It is inscribed, "& Grand-dad too? Laurie & Leslie."

Here is a grouping of more common classroom-style valentine cards, all showing cats or kittens.

"PLANE" AS CAN BE VALENTINE

HELLO THERE VALENTINE!

NO FOOLING I'M DROOLING OVER YOU VALENTINE!

To the Sweetest One of All

MADE IN U.S.A.

This kitty card made in the U.S.A. is inscribed, "From Rachel."

To my Valentine

This rare kitty valentine card has glass eyes and is mechanical. It was printed in Germany in the early 1900s.

This 1937 valentine states, "I'm getting in my licks now—be my valentine." It is inscribed, "To Rena, From Otis."

These three kitty valentines all pull out to offer a surprise.

Scotty valentines came in a variety of sizes.

TO MY VALENTINE

TO MY VALENTINE

I LIKE 'EM FRIENDLY,
I LIKE 'EM TRUE,
I LIKE 'EM HAPPY,
JUST LIKE YOU.

from Happy

I PUP-POSE TO BE YOUR VALENTINE

WHAT A "PICNIC" FOR ME, IF YOU WERE MY VALENTINE

The use of puppies was popular on children's valentine cards. Here are two examples.

HOWLING MY VALENTINE

VALENTINE

My Valentine, COULD YOU REMEMBER TO—

SQUEEZE IN A LITTLE TIME FOR ME?

This is a great grouping of class-room-style valentine cards showing a variety of puppies.

If there were means by which I knew— YOUR heart was acting queerly, too!

HEART BEAT RECEIVING SET

Love
Ole

Wow! What is this puppy up to? This fun valentine card was made in the U.S.A.

TO MY VALENTINE

My heart keeps going "PIT-A-PAT", And I would not object to THAT—

MY VALENTINE

WATCH OUT! Why waste TIME

Not many valentines show dogs and cats together. But this one does.

when I'm ready to be one of your BIG MOMENTS!

Perhaps a song for your valentine? This card reads on the back, "Listen Valentine, I have a little secret To whisper in your ear, Of all the folks I ever knew, I love you best—my dear." It is marked, "Carrington Co. Chicago, Ill." It is inscribed, "To Rena Mae From Georgia."

This rare early-1900s, German foldout valentine card gives a 3-D look when pulled out.

You can open or move these valentines
to see what you'll be getting!

LOVE

IT WILL BE THE "LAST STRAW" IF

GETTING READY to be your VALENTINE

POWDER

YOU WON'T BE MY VALENTINE !

From Margaret Hamilton

I'M ALL DRESSED UP
AND FEELING FINE—
WAITING FOR YOU
DEAR VALENTINE!

I LOVE YOU

Valentine

Bunnies were used quite frequently on children's Valentine's Day cards.

YOU'RE MY "PET" VALENTINE!

You Took My HEART

AUTO
VALENTINE

Just "BECOWS"

OH VALENTINE!

YOU'RE A MASTERPIECE OF A VALENTINE

I LIKE YOU I'D BE

"MOUSE" you be so shy? I'd SHOOT THE WORKS

BE MY VALENTINE

HANG IT ALL YOU'RE MONKEYING WITH

Go CONTENTED TO BE YOUR VALENTINE

My Valentine

DON'T BE SUCH AN OLD "SOFTIE"

MY HEART

All the animals in the zoo are on these valentines! What an array, from bears to mice to cows. These types of cards were very popular with children then and now.

I COULDN'T **BEAR** TO LOSE YOU

DEAR Valentine

DEAR VALENTINE Don't let some POOR FISH run away with YOUR HEART!

To My Valentine

*German Valentine's Day cards like this one from 1930 used
bright colors to set off the beauty of the design.*

BIBLIOGRAPHY

Asala, Joanne. *Celtic Folklore Cooking.* St. Paul: Llewellyn, 1998.

Barth, Edna. *Hearts, Cupids, and Red Roses: The Story of the Valentine Symbols.* New York: Seasbury Press, 1974.

Bridell Fradin, Dennis. *Valentine's Day.* Springfield, N.J.: Enslow Publishers, 1990.

Brown, Fern. *Valentine's Day.* New York: Franklin Watts, 1983.

Copycat Magazine (January/February 1996).

Dresser, Norine. *Multicultural Manners: New Rules of Etiquette for a Changing Society.* New York: John Wiley and Sons, 1996.

Krythe, Maymie. *All About American Holidays.* New York: Harper and Row, 1962.

Newshouse News Service (February 1992).

Spicer, Dorothy Gladys. *The Book of Festivals.* Detroit: Gale Research, 1964.

USA Today (February 2001).

OTHER SOURCES

Antique Trader
Antique Weekly
Knoxville (Tenn.) Library
Seymour (Tenn.) Herald
U.S. Department of Agriculture
U.S. Census